Guardian of the Flame
The Story of Hospital Point Lighthouse Keeper Joseph Henry Herrick

Edward R. Brown

Beverly Historical Society
Beverly, Massachusetts

Copyright © 2016 by Beverly Historical Society

All rights reserved. This book or any portion thereof may not be reproduced or used in any manner whatsoever without the express written permission of the publisher except for the use of brief quotations in a book review or scholarly journal.

First Printing: 2016

ISBN 1-891906-14-3

Beverly Historical Society
117 Cabot Street
Beverly, MA 01915

www.beverlyhistory.org

Ordering Information: Special discounts are available on quantity purchases by corporations, associations, educators, and others. For details, contact the publisher at the above listed address.

U.S. trade bookstores and wholesalers: Please contact Beverly Historical Society, 978-922-1186; or email info@beverlyhistory.org

Contents

Preface 4

Chapter 1: A True Son of Beverly 6

Chapter 2: Lighthouse Keeper 13

Chapter 3: Retirement, Sunset and Evening Star 25

Appendix 1: Hospital Point Chronology 31

Appendix 2: Keepers of the Lighthouse 1871 - 1947 34

Appendix 3: Misery Loves Company 37

Appendix 4: The "Other" Joseph Henry Herrick 39

U.S. Coast Guard Auxiliary: A Proud Tradition, A Worthy Mission 43

Foreword

The name of Joseph Henry Herrick is hardly remembered in conversations among Beverly historians, and it's safe to say that most residents of the community wouldn't recognize him at all. But this descendant of Beverly pioneers spent more than 43 years as keeper of Beverly's only lighthouse, the picturesque Hospital Point beacon with its adjoining house -- now the home of the commander of the First U.S. Coast Guard District – that has been so often photographed. The light had only five keepers in the 76 years between its installation and its automation in 1947, with Joseph Herrick's tenure being by far the longest. In that 43-plus years of dedicated service – get this – keeper Herrick NEVER received a pay raise from his federal employer, the U.S. Lighthouse Service, while never missing a full day of work and raising a family in the keeper's house. He said that his salary was the same when he retired in 1917 as it was in 1874, save for the addition of a minuscule subsistence stipend. But while the government agency may have taken him for granted, chances are that many a mariner owed a debt of thanks, if not his life, to the keeper of the beacon that guided them through shoal, storm and fog to a safe anchorage.

Before entering the federal service, Joseph Herrick was a shoemaker in Beverly. He was a Union soldier in the Civil War, but luckily for him never had to serve more than ten miles from home! Several of the lighthouse journals that Joseph Herrick kept are now in the possession of the Beverly Historical Society (BHS). Besides the routine weather entries, they include notes on many fascinating happenings both at sea and in his home town. This modest man, described as "genial" by a local newspaper reporter, entered the names of practically everyone who visited his lighthouse. But never once did he write his own name in the journal volume, so unless readers of the journals care to dig around for the facts, they'll never know who the keeper was.

Joseph Henry Herrick lived to the age of 90, and except for the 190 days of his military service never resided away from the town of his birth. Sadly, we don't know what he looked like. It's disappointing that even the extensive front page story that led the *Beverly Evening Times* on the day of his retirement failed to include a likeness or even a physical description of the then 80-year-old pillar of the community. He joined John Hale Chipman Post 89 of the Grand Army of the Republic (GAR) when it was organized late in 1868, but to our disappointment his photo is not in the BHS's extensive GAR files. A pencil notation on his sheet in the Beverly post's Memorial Record book reads "Dropped 1876." No explanation was added. Perhaps his lighthouse duties precluded veterans' activities, or maybe he felt embarrassed at being a "stay at home" veteran among men who had seen war at its worst. We can't tell, but unfortunately he wasn't involved when a photographer later took pictures of the Chipman Post members.

This is his story.

E.R.B.

Circa 1873. Glass plate negative.

A TRUE SON OF BEVERLY

Our heritage is strong, and as the years go by
Its luster grows more mellow – we all know
It will remain unchanged each day that passes,
And our future will be brightened by its glow."

– From "Our Heritage," by Beatrice Stone
Written for Beverly's Tercentenary Celebration, 1968

Joseph Henry Herrick was born in Beverly on 25 July 1837, the son of Emerson and Huldah (Butman) Herrick, who were married here on 31 May 1831. Until just before the turn of the 20th century he called himself Joseph Henry Herrick 2nd to distinguish himself from an uncle of the same name, born 31 October 1812, son of Thomas and Mary (Greely) Herrick. What is interesting is that through the Beverly Vital Records it is easy to trace his ancestry and determine that he's a seventh generation direct descendant of one of Beverly's founding families, a family that stayed in Beverly through the years. Emerson Herrick's parents were the above mentioned Thomas Herrick, born 24 March 1773, and Mary Greely, daughter of Nicholas Greely. Our hero's paternal great-grandparents were Henry Herrick, born 1741, and Mary (Foster). His second great-grandparents were William, born 1709, and Mary (Tuck). Continuing the line back to the 17th century we have Henry, born 1671 or 1672 in Beverly and his wife Susanna Beadle; Zachariah Herrick, born in 1636 and who married Mary Dodge; and finally the pioneer, old Henry, born 16 August 1604 in Loughborough, Leicestershire, England, who migrated to the new world with his wife Edith Laskin of Dorsetshire, and who died here in 1671. The future lighthouse keeper was in every way a native son of Beverly. Whether he was aware of his ancestral line is unknown, and he didn't boast about it on the one occasion when he was visited by a reporter.

Both the retirement story and a brief account of his death that appeared on the front page of the Beverly Times on 17 October 1927 say only that Joseph Herrick was educated in the Beverly public schools. Beverly had a number of district schools when he was a boy, but we don't know which one he would have attended. The town didn't have a high school until 1858.

For a brief glimpse of what his schooling might have been like we can turn to the "most recent" history of Beverly, written by Edwin Stone in 1843 when little Joseph was six and starting his formal education. We're told that in 1841 Beverly had 1249 young people between the ages of four and sixteen and that the town boasted of ten schoolhouses, all but one of which had been erected "before public education was awakened," but which were nevertheless, in Stone's words, "commodious and in good condition." The average school population that year was 593 in winter and 504 in summer, which again gives the lie to the oft-repeated myth that the current school year with its summer vacation is a "relic of the agricultural economy." There was no grade system as yet, but children could advance as their skills improved. They apparently could choose the winter term, summer term or both.

Beverly at the time had a school committee, which voted in 1836 to adopt the following books for use in the public schools. This list, which obviously includes texts for both primary and older pupils and would hardly pass muster in the 21st century, included: *Cummings' Spelling Book, the New Testament, Young Readers Introduction to The National Reader, The National Reader, Sullivan's Political Class Book, Woodbridge's Geography and Atlas, Colburn's Arithmetic, Goodrich's History of the United States, Comstock's Philosophy,*

Holbrook's Geometry, Fowle's Linear Drawing, Blair's Rhetoric, Colburn's Algebra, Bowditch's Navigator (surely of use to a future lighthouse keeper), *Worcester's Dictionary, Story's Abridgement, Parker's Natural Philosophy*, and *Greenleaf's Arithmetic*, with other volumes added as they became available. It is easy to see that, assuming young Joseph continued his formal schooling until the age of 13 or 14, when most youngsters began their working life, he would have been exposed to a basic knowledge of all the subjects necessary for a youth with ambition, though without the added benefit of higher education, to make a good living in the 19th century.

When school was over for the lad in the early 1850s, the surviving accounts indicate that he went to work as a shoemaker (or cordwainer), a trade that was very popular in 19th century Beverly. The writer of his retirement story related that Herrick "was educated in the Beverly schools and when a lad went to making shoes, his first employment being with Neal Woodbury." Young Joseph also tried his hand at learning the grocery business as a clerk at the store at Cabot and Charnock streets, owned by Robert Whipple and Varnum Pedrick. But it would be shoemaking that he'd choose for employment until he was well into his 30s. Before and after the Civil War he was employed at the Israel Foster & Co. shoe factory, located on Rantoul Street at the corner of Railroad Avenue. Through those years he appears to have lived with his parents.

With the Confederate attack on Fort Sumter in April of 1861 that launched the bitter Civil War of North vs. South, men from Beverly flocked to the Union colors. The 8th Massachusetts Regiment, Company E, made up almost entirely of Beverly men, marched off almost immediately for a year of service. (Most people back home thought the war would be over long before then, instead of dragging on for four terrible years.) When the year was up, the men of the 8th agreed to re-enlist for another year, to prevent the need for a draft back home. But in the summer of 1863, after the decisive Union victory at Gettysburg in early July that blunted Confederate commander Robert E. Lee's plan to bring the war to the North, the 8th decided it had done its part, came home and was mustered out on August 7.

Many Beverly men participated with other military units through the end of the war in 1865, and many of Joseph Herrick's contemporaries went off early to war, but for whatever reason he chose not to enlist at that time. He did, however, put on the Union Army uniform in May of 1864. His name can be found, on the roster of the Second Unattached Company of the Massachusetts Volunteer Militia (Infantry), which was mustered into Federal service on 5 May 1864, with a 90-day enlistment. Its captain was Francis E. Porter, of Beverly, shoe manufacturer, a veteran of the early years of the war with the 8th Massachusetts. The first lieutenant was another old soldier from Beverly, Hugh Munsey, whose dress uniform and sword are part of the BHS collection. Second lieutenant was Eleazer Giles of Beverly, and the first sergeant was another Herrick from Beverly, cordwainer Benjamin. Most of the private soldiers in the company were Beverly men, the majority of them listed as cordwainers like Joseph H. Herrick. Although many were youths of 18 or 19, the roster also included such veterans of the earlier campaigns as John Hanners and Josiah K. Hull, whose Civil War drum resides in the collection of the Beverly Historical Society and Museum. Joseph H. Herrick, age 26, cordwainer, was making his debut as a soldier.

At first glance it might seem odd that 90-day enlistments were being accepted three years into the costly war, at a time when the armies of Ulysses S. Grant and Robert E. Lee were preparing to fight it out with terrible losses in the carnage of Spottsylvania and the Wilderness. But information contained in Volume 5 of *Massachusetts Soldiers, Sailors and Marines in the Civil War* clarifies the situation. These men were not to be sent to bolster Grant's and Meade's Army of the Potomac in Virginia, but rather ten miles north and east to neighboring Gloucester, Massachusetts. To throw further light on the subject, we turn to a 1972 reprint of John J. Babson's 1860 *History of the Town of Gloucester*. The editors included a historical review of events in the town since Babson compiled his volume. Believe it or not, Gloucester in 1864 was in fear of a Confederate attack and wanted military protection. Some months before, a rogue Rebel raider named the ***Tacony*** had attacked the Gloucester fishing fleet on George's Bank. After taking off the crews, the raiders then sank the boats. Word later reached Gloucester; the town was in a passion of rage and fear. Hurried appeals were made to Washington, which sent three Navy vessels in search of the ***Tacony***. To prevent any Confederate attacks on the coast, nine companies of Massachusetts militia would be brought to full strength with additional volunteers, mustered into U.S. service, and assigned to guard strategic coastal points. Capt. Porter's company would be stationed close to home, in nervous Gloucester.

Another local connection comes into play here. The old fortification at Stage Fort was reactivated and named Fort Conant, in honor of Beverly founder Roger Conant who had been governor of the abortive fishing colony at Cape Ann from 1623-26. From *The Proceedings of the Essex Institute* we learn that august body of Essex County historians made the suggestion for the fort's new name. A letter from Washington dated Feb. 7, 1864, signed by William Whiting, solicitor of the War Department, and addressed to Robert S. Rantoul Esq., reads as follows: "I have the pleasure of enclosing the order of the Secretary of War made at my request in accordance with the wishes of the Essex Institute, naming Fort Glover and Fort Conant." So the Beverly soldiers would be on duty at a place named for perhaps the most illustrious citizen of their home town in the 17th century. Conant had been picked in 1623 by the sponsoring company to govern what was hoped would be a successful fishing colony at what later became Gloucester. Unfortunately, most of the men picked to serve under him were worthless. Some were lazy, some were drunkards, some well intentioned but with no knowledge of how to extract fish from the Atlantic coastal waters. When the disappointed sponsors pulled the plug on the settlement in 1626, most of the men returned to England. But Conant and a small number of his best men, including John Balch, headed south and west with their families in search of a new place to settle.

They picked the seaside spot called by the Indian name of Naumkeag, soon re-christened Salem, and settled in, with Conant retaining the title of governor. He'd lose that title in 1628 when John Endicott arrived with the New England Company patent and some badly needed reinforcements for the struggling little settlement. The newcomers in turn had to give way two years later when John Winthrop's fleet sailed in with the liberal charter of the Massachusetts Bay Company. Winthrop would choose Boston as the site for his new capital, leaving Endicott, Charles Gott and others to take care of business in Salem. Conant moved across the water to what was then called Bass River Side, a village that would in 1668 turn into the town of Beverly.

Duty at Fort Conant must have been excruciatingly boring, as the men scanned the harbor for a phantom Rebel assault. At least it was far more comfortable and safer than the killing fields of Virginia. But when their 90 day enlistment expired and they were officially mustered out on August 6, everyone including Joseph H. Herrick agreed to sign on the next day for a new period of 100 days of service. By mid-November it was obvious that Gloucester and the other coastal towns were safe from invasion. By then the southern Confederacy was reeling. Gen. William T. Sherman had burned Atlanta and was "making Georgia howl" on his march to the sea. Gen. George Thomas was about to put the finishing touches on the remaining Rebel army in Tennessee. Grant and Lee had settled down to their bitter winter stalemate outside Petersburg, a stalemate that in early spring of '65 would be broken by the Union victory at Five Forks, followed by Lee's surrender a few days later. By November, the Beverly soldiers must have been eager for home and hearth. For nearly another decade, Joseph H. Herrick's occupation would continue to be shoemaker, making his home with his parents. But all that was about to change.

C. 1893. Photograph by Lizzie Mitchell.

LIGHTHOUSE KEEPER

Let the lower lights be burning!
Send a gleam across the wave
Some poor fainting, struggling seaman
You may rescue, you may save"

– From 1871 hymn by Philip P. Bliss
– Public domain

Be dressed for action and have your lamps lit

– Luke 12:35

We don't know how the humble shoemaker Joseph Henry Herrick 2nd came to be recruited by the U.S. Lighthouse Service, which until its absorption by the Coast Guard in 1939 was responsible for all manned lighthouses on the ocean and the Great Lakes. Herrick's retirement story, which refers to him as "Capt. Herrick," (seemingly an honorary title awarded by the Lighthouse Service) gives no answer to that question. Local records of the time are ambiguous, at best. The earliest town directories at the Beverly Historical Society, published in 1875 and 1877, show Herrick's occupation to be shoemaker, even though by then he had been lighthouse keeper for some time. Emerson Herrick, no occupation, is listed as having a house at Hospital Point, with his son as a boarder. Perhaps the compiler of the directory took it for granted that the older man was the householder and his son was a boarder, when in fact it might actually have been the other way around. Emerson Herrick, age about 70, certainly never kept the lighthouse. At this distance it is impossible to sort it out. Huldah Herrick, Joseph's mother and apparently then a widow, was living with him in 1882, but is gone two years later. In the 1870 Federal Census

Joseph H. Herrick is single, age 33, shoemaker, living with Emerson, then 64, and Huldah. 62.

There's another discrepancy, too. According to the *Beverly Times* story, Herrick was made keeper of the Hospital Point lighthouse on Nov. 3, 1874. But the first entry in the oldest journal at the BHS, which seems plainly to be in Herrick's writing, is dated almost a year earlier, Nov. 11, 1873. It is possible, of course, that JHH's first year of duty was a probationary period and his appointment as keeper not made "official" until 1874, but there is nothing in the journal to throw any light on that speculation. What we do know is that in 1870, at the request of the Lighthouse Board, the U.S. Congress approved an appropriation of $30,000 to improve safety around Salem Harbor by building three lighthouses – at Derby Wharf and Winter Island (Fort Pickering) in Salem, and at Hospital Point in Beverly. These would augment the existing lights (originally two) on Baker's Island. They were considered essential to guard the narrow deep water channel that provided safe access to the inner harbor. A temporary light was erected at Hospital Point in 1871, followed the next year by the permanent, current tower standing 70 feet above sea level, and the neat, two-story keeper's house next door. The first appointed keeper was William Augustus Friend, who from published information appears to have been known by his middle name. He cannot have stayed more than two years in the position, and seems to have left Beverly after turning the lighthouse over to the successor who wouldn't retire until 1917.

Joseph Henry Herrick remained a bachelor until his late 30s. But when he did marry, it is perhaps not surprising that he chose Joanna W. Haskell, a member of another established local family that also dates back to the 17th century. She was born in Beverly on 26 June, 1850, the daughter of John and Clarissa (Sargent) Haskell, whose marriage intentions were filed here on 22 Nov. 1835. The date of the

Herrick-Haskell wedding has not been found, but most likely it was in 1875, when he would have been 38 and she 25. Joanna moved into the keeper's house which would be her home for about 42 years, and she must have quickly fallen into the routine of being a lighthouse keeper's wife and number one helper. They wasted little time in starting a family. A son, christened Arthur Sargent Herrick, was born to them in 1876. The 1880 census lists him as being 4 years old, son of Joseph, lighthouse keeper, and Joanna, housewife. After a gap of 12 years, a daughter, Clara, would be born in 1888 to complete the family. She might have come as something of a surprise, since her father was past 50, her mother 38, and her brother closing in on his teens.

Herrick's lighthouse was equipped with a 3½ order Fresnel (pronounced FREE-nel) lens. There were seven orders of Fresnel lenses, and according to Jeremy D'Entremont, author of *The Lighthouses of Massachusetts*, that particular model is rare in New England. The lens was invented in 1822 by the French physicist Augustine Fresnel, and it soon became the most popular installation for lighthouse service. To explain it in the simplest terms, a series of glass prisms is employed to bend light into a narrow beam. Fresnel's highly efficient lens could capture up to 83 percent of the light generated by the lamp, so the beam could be seen 20 or more miles to the horizon.

And Hospital Point Light had a feature that was, according to Jeremy D'Entremont, "considered unique in American lighthouses." It was designed to vastly improve the safety of mariners at night. That feature was a condensing panel installed in front of the lens. From viewing a photo of this feature, it appears to be made of several attached glass panels extending about three-quarters of the way to the top of the lens. Ships entering the harbor, once they have negotiated the tricky passage between Baker's and Misery islands, have to work their way through a channel between dangerous rocky breakers and ledges, sometimes hard to see at night. When mariners pick up Hospital Point Light, the trick is to make sure to steer so that they always can see the beam at full brightness. That's where the condensing panel comes in. It's designed so that should the helmsman veer away from the main channel, the beam will suddenly diminish in intensity. When that happens, it's essential to make a quick correction with the wheel or tiller and regain the beam before the vessel strays into possible trouble. Over the years this lens undoubtedly has prevented many a shipwreck.

For Joseph H. Herrick and his fellow lighthouse keepers, the job involved sticking to a strict routine. There were no days off, even for illness, unless the keeper was lucky enough to have an assistant (not the case for a smaller station like Beverly's), or a wife who knew the routine as well as he did. The oil lamp had to be lighted at sundown and extinguished at sunrise. Keepers conditioned themselves to awaken every couple of hours to make sure the light was working properly. Arrival of a thick fog during daylight hours also meant lighting the lamp. It was the keeper's sworn responsibility to keep things in order no matter what. On a night when it was ten degrees above zero, blowing a gale, and a keeper was sick enough to keep most people in bed, he still had to climb the swaying ladder to the top of the tower in order to trim the wick and refill the oil reservoir. There were many routine maintenance chores that had to be performed every day without fail. Besides attending to the lamp, the lens and the oil supply, there was brasswork to be polished, one of the banes of a lighthouse keeper's life. More than likely the Herrick children, growing up at the lighthouse, would have pitched in to help with the daily chores. Every three months the station was inspected by an officer of the Lighthouse Service. JHH seems always to have secured high marks on those inspections, all of which he faithfully entered into his journal along with the inspecting officer's signature. He never entered his own name, however. Unlike keepers at lonely, isolated stations, the Herricks at least were fortunate to be serving at a lighthouse only about two miles from the center of their familiar hometown.

On a sunny day, when the chores were done, the keeper and his family might slip away for a couple of hours to visit friends, do some shopping, take part in a meeting, witness a local veterans parade or attend worship. According to a story published on the day of his death, Herrick was a member of the Dane Street Congregational Church, and he also joined the Bass River Lodge of Odd Fellows, of which he was a member for more than 50 years. One day early in his tenure, Herrick wrote, he had to go to Boston to draw his pay. More than likely he would have taken one of the Eastern Railroad's steam trains on that occasion. If the keeper's house was deserted for an hour or two, the man in charge would just have to hope that no "official" visitor picked that time to drop in unexpectedly. The Hospital Point Light was furnished with supplies delivered regularly by a steamer in the employ of the Lighthouse Service. Herrick frequently mentioned visits by the "Daisy" or the "Fern."

For nearly his entire career, Joseph Henry Herrick maintained the same oil-fired lamp. But in 1916, just a year before he retired, the Lighthouse Service changed Hospital Point to a new light source, using incandescent oil vapor (IOV). According to an on-line source, an IOV system was first tried in Europe in the 1880s and 1890s with little success. In 1901, an American, Arthur Kitson, came up with an improved version. But it was the "triple mantle" IOV perfected in 1904 by Sir Thomas Matthews in England that the U.S. Lighthouse Service began to test with success in 1913. It was a complex system using a kerosene pressure tank, a "spirit lamp," and a copper heat retainer to vaporize the kerosene. Unfortunately we have no idea of what JHH thought of this new arrangement, since the journal of his last years on the job has not turned up. You'd have to suspect that after so many years of doing things "by the book" the same way, at age 79 he might not have welcomed learning to deal with a completely new and complicated device.

It is in those journals that he so carefully kept and which have so thankfully been preserved that we can best connect with the old lighthouse keeper through his own words. On most days the entries were routine weather observations and records of visitors. But not all of his observations were routine. One September day in 1882 he took count of the unusually heavy traffic lying at anchor. "Sept. 25 1882. One hundred and twenty five vessels anchored in Salem Harbor nearly one week, waiting for the storm to be over and for fair winds."

Unusual sights came in for comment. "March 5, 1882. The first water bicycle passed in the vicinity. Two of them passed by as far as Misery Island and returned again to the harbor." Nobody at the BHS was familiar with the term water bicycle. But we have since learned that at least one manufacturer now offers a modern version of a device that must have been similar to the ones that fascinated JHH as he watched from the lighthouse. The water bicycle, bearing US patent #5316508, is described as having "two steerable front pontoons and two rear pontoons fixed to a main frame, substantially similar to a conventional bicycle frame. Handlebars are provided to turn the steerable front pontoons. . .The water bicycle has a pedal mechanism and a bicycle-type transmission powering a propeller located at the rear." JHH must have smiled as he watched the merry cyclists pedal their previously unseen devices out to the harbor island, loop around and return to their starting point. It must have been great exercise. But anyone who ventured onto ocean waters, even close to shore, on a water bicycle would have been well advised to keep a sharp eye on the horizon for any sign of an approaching squall or fog bank. The device most likely would easily swamp in a heavy sea, and would be hard to pedal against a strong wind.

Fires always attracted the keeper's attention. "April 23, 1882. A great conflagration in Salem which burned the jute delivered by the ship **Memnon**." Jute, a plant imported from Asia, yielded a fiber used in the manufacture of rope and burlap. (The **Memnon** had passed the lighthouse inbound a week earlier.) Watching from the lighthouse, Herrick must have had a grand view of that blaze, which was reported in the Monday, April 24 issue of the *Salem Register* under the headline "Fire On Phillips Wharf." The fire was reported by telephone on Sunday the 23rd at 5:30 pm: "The fire department mustered promptly, but the inflammable nature of the material in the building caused the fire to spread with astonishing rapidity, and the wooden building in which it originated, together with the granite storehouse adjoining, were totally destroyed. The first building was 100 feet by 25 feet, built in 1871, and contained about 700 bales of jute just discharged from the ship **Memnon**." The buildings were owned by the Boston and Lowell Railroad Co. (which built a spur line to Phillips Wharf); the jute and other goods by the Nevins Baggage Co. The *Register* said the losses probably were covered by insurance. "Incendiarism is suspected" as cause of the blaze, fought by three Salem steam pumpers and one from Peabody. "June 4, 1903. Forest fires raging all around causing the sky to look yellow."

While the keeper prided himself on the condition of his light, mishaps occurred from time to time and he didn't shrink from mentioning them, especially since others might have noticed them. "April 7, 1882. Lighthouse out 20 minutes between 7 and 8 o'clock, cause the supply tube filled up with dirt." One can imagine Herrick struggling to clear the offending tube, and berating himself for not noticing the defect earlier. It wasn't long until the light was shining brightly again, but a keeper might consider 20 minutes of down time a mark against his diligence.

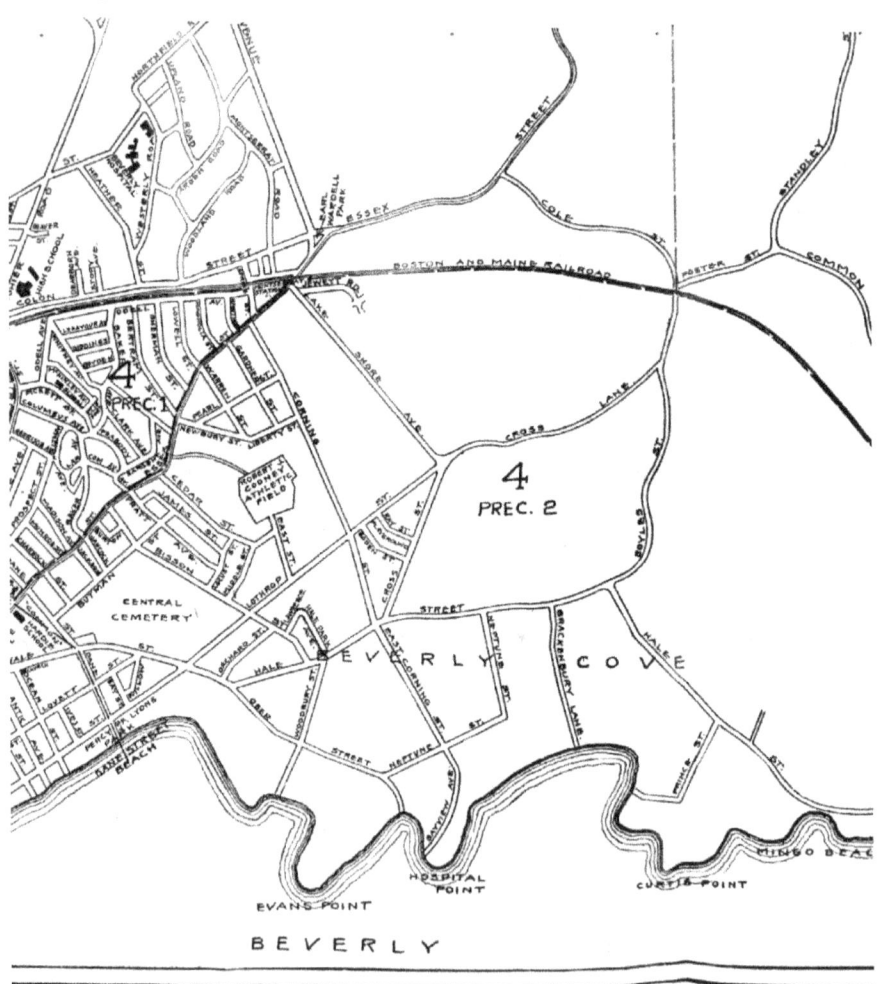

Events taking place in his home town found their way into the keeper's journal. Although he was no longer active in the Beverly GAR post, JHH was on hand for one of the most noteworthy local events of the 1880s, dedication of Beverly's spectacular Civil War memorial, paid for by public subscription, erected opposite Central Fire Station at what is now Monument Square. Herrick described the scene, which attracted participants and spectators from many neighboring towns, this way: "Oct. 13, 1882. Dedication of the Soldiers Monument took place in town. It is estimated ten thousand persons were present. The procession consisted of nearly all the GAR posts in this county, also Odd Fellows and all the Catholic Temperance organizations and all the Firemen in Beverly." Herrick also noted that on May 30 he took the afternoon off to attend Memorial Day observances in town, returning to the lighthouse at 5 p.m.

Although JHH's job was to prevent shipwrecks, there were tragedies in the harbor waters which he was helpless to avert, and which he recorded with a touch of sadness.

Oct. 22, 1881. A sad drowning incident occurred off the Middle Breakers. Frank B. Wallis and Powell Mason were swamped in a dory. Wallis was saved, Mason was drowned. Unsuccessful efforts to find the body have been made. A reward of 500 dollars has been offered." Despite the incentive of what was for the time a huge reward by a grieving family anxious to conduct a burial service, Herrick added a note on Oct. 31 that "the body of Mason has not been found."

June 15, 1903. Harold Sweetser drowned off Misery Island by breaking rail of steam launch. Capt. and engineer saved." At that time the short-lived summer colony on Misery Island was thriving. The company owned a steam launch that ran between the island and the pier at West Beach in Beverly Farms. Herrick later added a journal note that the body of "young Sweetser" had been found floating off Misery Island. Another tragedy that he looked back on at the time of his retirement was the "Surf City" disaster of July 4, 1898. The excursion steamer was hit by a sudden thunder squall as it carried holiday revelers on a harbor cruise. Eight persons were drowned, but many other lives were saved thanks to the heroism of witnesses from shore who rushed to the scene aboard any boat they could reach.

But there were happier incidents to report, including the arrival of an important new neighbor. "July 4, 1909. President Taft arrived at the Stetson Cottage for the summer." "Sept. 11, 1909. Essex County parade of the Grand Army. Reviewed by Pres. Taft." "May 18, 1910. Halley's Comet plainly visible in the eastern sky." "Aug. 31, 1910. Pres. Taft laid cornerstone of the YMCA building." "Sept. 17, 1910. Very brilliant sunset and a perfect rainbow."

Then there was the weather. Herrick rarely omitted an entry for each day. His favorite word, when a day was calm and serene, was "pleasant." But of course there were days that were far from pleasant. "July 30, 1903. Two very severe thunderstorms visited this vicinity, most severe for years. Lightning struck a number of places." "Oct. 10, 1903. Very severe gale of wind and rain continuing three days, does a great deal of damage. Morrison's gasoline yacht came ashore and smashed in pieces."

Of course, winter brought a variety of challenges. Perhaps the "mother" of all New England winters occurred in 1875, and it was one to which for many years future winters would be compared. It was so cold that year that the harbor froze all the way out to Baker's Island. But there was a triumphant moment when "Captain Keene, who was feared lost, came in with the **Sarah H. Putnam**." With the vessel unable to reach the harbor due to the ice, rescuers pushed a dory over the ice "from Crowell's Wharf to Baker's Island, where the captain and his crew were given a royal welcome." That year, Herrick saw two men walk on the ice to Misery Island and back.

Talk about contrasting New England winters. Herrick's journal compared the season of 1904 with one that occurred just two years later.

1904 – "Jan. 31. January a very cold and disagreeable month with much snow. The most cold since 1875." "March 20 (first day of spring). Much snow on ground. Winter of 1904 was most severe for years, very cold and very much snow." And it wasn't over, by any means, as April would bring more of the bitter winter weather experienced over the previous four months. "April 15. Quite a heavy snowstorm. In some places cars" (whether this meant trolleys or steam trains is uncertain) "were unable to run. Stormy all over New England and New York." Did that mid-April pounding mean that winter finally was through? No! "April 20 and 21. Quite a heavy fall of snow for the time of year." (JHH seems to have written those words with tongue a bit in cheek.) Finally, starting on April 27, "3 days very heavy rain" washed it all away. That must have caused considerable flooding, but at least in those days most of the wetlands hadn't been displaced for building construction.

1906 – On Jan. 19, JHH wrote that he had "picked a very nice dandelion on the hill under the locust." "Jan. 21. Thermometer standing at 72 degrees, as nice as any summer day." "Feb. 28. Feb. was a very uncommon warm month. Crocuses, hepaticas and other spring flowers were picked on Feb. 22. Winter of '06 was warmest ever known."

Joseph Herrick always had his family by his side. After he married Joanna and brought her to the lighthouse cottage, she would be his faithful helpmeet for the rest of his 42 years of service there. Son Arthur, like his father, would wait until his mid-30s to marry. In 1910, at age 34, he was living at Hospital Point with his parents. (In 1897, at 21 he had been a farm worker.) He later took a job with the City of Beverly as a laborer in the Public Works Department. By the time his father left the lighthouse, Arthur was married and was building a house at 12 Boden St., beside the Cove Playground (now known officially as Kimball Haskell Park). Clara, who never married, stayed with her parents all their lives.

c. 1905. Note the woman in the center of the image.

RETIREMENT, SUNSET AND EVENING STAR

I dig, scrub and polish and work with a might
And just when I get it all shiny and bright
In comes the fog like a thief in the night
Goodbye brasswork

And when I have polished until I am cold
And I'm taken aloft to the Heavenly fold
Will my harp and my crown be made of pure gold?
No, brasswork

– From "Brasswork, Or the Lighthouse Keeper's Lament"
– Author unknown

The July 15, 1917 edition of the *Beverly Evening Times* featured a lengthy front page story headlined, "After 43 Years Of Faithful Service, Capt. Herrick Quits Lighthouse." American soldiers, Beverly boys among them, by then were being dispatched by troop ship to France to fight alongside our British and French allies against Kaiser Wilhelm's German invaders. But the lead story that mid-July day in the local daily paper told of the retirement of Joseph H. Herrick. The writer of the piece is unknown. Reporters in those days didn't normally sign their stories, and editors seldom bestowed bylines. The Herrick story was so long that it "jumped" from page 1 to page 8. Readers were informed that having nearly reached the age of 80, Beverly's veteran lighthouse keeper decided that the time had come for him to surrender his duties. Whether installation of the newfangled IOV system contributed to his decision to retire is hard to say.

JHH had notified the Lighthouse Service of his intention to retire on June 30, 1917, about a month shy of his 80th birthday. His employers, however, according to the story, persuaded him to stay on until July 15. The *Times* gave no reason for this, but one can conclude that the Lighthouse Service needed extra time to move Levi B. Clark, the man picked to take over at Hospital Point, to Beverly from his post on remote Cuttyhunk Island. (Clark's name, or anything about a successor, is never mentioned in the story.) In his 43 years of service, said the *Times*, Herrick "has seen many changes on the shore." The writer added: "Those who have visited the lighthouse enjoyed the hospitality of the Herrick home by the sea." Joanna liked to bake, and according to the story neighborhood children loved to drop by the lighthouse cottage to enjoy one of her cookies.

Herrick was made lighthouse keeper in 1874, "and has been tending the light ever since, lighting it at sunset and extinguishing it at sunrise." The most stunning revelation in the story is that the just retired keeper informed the *Times* that in his 43 years of unbroken and faithful service, "he has never had a raise in salary." A few years before, "the government gave orders that the lighthouse keepers were to be given ration money, 35 cents a day." In the only direct quote attributed to the "genial captain," Herrick noted that "this doesn't go very far these days." It would be the first time the couple had ever moved, and Joanna told the reporter, "I hope it's the last time." (It would be.) "For the family," said the *Times* writer, "there is the regret of having to leave the pretty house that has been theirs for years." At least they wouldn't have to move very far. Despite the parsimony of his government employer, JHH had saved enough money from his salary to build or purchase a house in the Cove a short distance from the lighthouse, at 12 Brackenbury Lane, which would be the Herricks' new home. "Buff the lighthouse cat" would be moving with them.

The rest of the story reveals little new information. He was "educated in the Beverly schools and then went to making shoes." There was a brief mention that he had served in the Civil War and joined the Chipman GAR Post, "and after the war went back to shoemaking for

Cover of "Beverly, Mass." published by Nathan H. Foster, early 20th century.

Israel Foster." The reporter didn't think to ask Herrick about how he came to join the Lighthouse Service. All in all it was a good piece about the sea change at Hospital Point.

How Joseph Henry Herrick passed the time in his retirement years is completely unknown. Some lighthouse keepers were artists or wood carvers, but there is no mention of Herrick having engaged in any hobbies. Even had he still belonged to the Chipman Post, by 1917 the long ranks of Civil War veterans had dwindled to a thin blue line. He might still have been a member of the Odd Fellows, but most of the friends he had made there over nearly a half century of membership were gone now. Probably there were still old friends to visit and reminisce with. While he may not have missed the drudgery and confinement of some of the lighthouse duties, there must have been times he wished he could once again light the faithful beacon that guided so many ships home. But his watch had passed.

There were no grandchildren to dote on. Clara Herrick never married. Arthur, who in 1910 was living at the lighthouse at age 34, took a bride on 15 February, 1911 according to the city clerk's statistics for that year. She was Annie C. Roberts. They lived first on Neptune Street, and Arthur worked as a gardener. In 1917, a new street was cut through connecting Cross and East Lothrop streets, running beside the Cove Playground. The first house on that street was built for Arthur and Annie Herrick. This road was at first called "Bowdoin Street" until the city settled on the spelling "Boden." A few years later Arthur had taken a job as laborer for the City of Beverly Public Works department, a job he kept until his retirement about 1945. There is no evidence that the couple had children. Annie died on 7 February 7, 1946 and Arthur on 7 March, 1947. No obituary for either has been located to confirm their childless status. Although Arthur was the only son of a prominent Beverlyite and had worked for the city more than 20 years, if the date of his death reported in the 1947 City Directory is correct, the *Beverly Times* did not publish a death notice or obituary on that day or any of the days to follow. But the lack of children seems to be confirmed by scanning the City Directories. It was customary that when a child reached the age of 17 or so, he or she would be listed as boarding at home. Nowhere from 1927 on is there any mention of any resident of 12 Boden Street other than Arthur and Annie.

Sadly, Joanna Herrick would have only four years to enjoy her new home on Brackenbury Lane. She passed away on 14 October 1921 at the age of 71, with burial in Central Cemetery according to her death certificate. Her husband lived to the age of 90, ten years after his retirement. A short story on the front page of the *Beverly Evening Times* on the 17th of October 1927, is headed: "Joseph H. Herrick Died This Morning." The story begins:

> Joseph H. Herrick, a well known and respected resident of Beverly Cove for many years died this morning at the advanced age of 90 years, and he was for more than forty-three

years keeper of the government light at Hospital Point until his retirement several years ago.

Born in Beverly, Capt. Herrick was educated in the Beverly schools and in his younger days clerked at Zachariah Cole's grocery store, corner Cabot and Charnock streets, and later took up the trade of a shoe worker. He was made the second keeper of Hospital Point light succeeding Augustus Friend. He made a splendid record as lighthouse keeper and had a wide circle of friends throughout the city. He leaves one daughter, Miss Clara Herrick and a son Arthur S. Herrick both of whom make their home in Beverly.

He had been a member of Bass River Lodge of Odd Fellows for over 50 years and was an attendant at the Dane Street Congregational church. He was a veteran of the Civil War. That's all. News of his death must have reached the *Times* office before any funeral arrangements were made. It was customary at that time for the paper to cover the funeral service of a well-known resident, but in subsequent days there was no story about his funeral or any information about a service, which presumably would have been held at the Dane Street Church.

After his death, Clara inherited the Brackenbury Lane home and lived there by herself for about another two decades. After Arthur Herrick passed away, Clara sold her parents' home (which has been continuously owned over the years by the Cucchiaro family) and moved to her late brother's home on Boden Street. If she inherited that dwelling it would be further evidence that her brother and sister-in-law were childless. She died there on 5 June 1971, age 83, the last of the "lighthouse Herricks."

Joseph Henry Herrick, a true son of "old Beverly," was a man who never sought the limelight, too modest even to write in own name in the lighthouse keeper's journal. But he is along with the entire Herrick clan, forever part of Beverly's heritage, and its history. Perhaps he'd be happy to know he isn't entirely forgotten.

APPENDIX ONE

HOSPITAL POINT CHRONOLOGY

18th century: Known as "Paul's Head" or "Thorndike's Point" for 17th century owner Paul Thorndike. In 1775, an artillery battery was established there, right after His Majesty's Schooner **Nautilus**, commanded by Capt. John Collins, had its celebrated encounter on 10 October 1775 with Gen. George Washington's armed vessel **Hannah**, commanded by Nick Broughton of Marblehead. The **Hannah** had sailed from Beverly earlier in the day and after encountering the much bigger **Nautilus** retreated to Beverly Harbor. This was probably the only time the town has ever received enemy fire. One of the cannon balls from the **Nautilus** is now owned by the Beverly Historical Society and Museum. Of further interest, as reported by author Thomas Macy in *The Hannah and the Nautilus* (Beverly Historical Society & Museum, 2002) is that Colonel Henry Herrick was in command of the Beverly militiamen who turned out that day to protect both their town and the heavily outmanned patriot ship that had sailed from Beverly. Both vessels were aground, but after a rising tide floated the Nautilus free, she withdrew to Boston.

1801: A smallpox hospital was built there to house victims during an epidemic of the dreaded disease. Victims removed there were cared for by persons who had been previously exposed to the contagious disease and were therefore immune. While a vaccine for smallpox had been introduced in Boston as early as 1720 and was promoted by Cotton Mather, resistance to vaccination remained strong among some people until well into the 19th century. After this, the name of the promontory was changed to Hospital Point.

1812: During the War of 1812, with fears of British naval assault on the coastal towns, the former hospital building was briefly converted to a military barracks.

1849: The building at Hospital Point is destroyed by fire.

1871: The U.S. Lighthouse Service erects a temporary beacon at Hospital Point. The following year, it is replaced by the familiar lighthouse and adjoining keeper's house.

1916: The original oil light is replaced by an incandescent oil vapor (IOV) lamp.

1927: An electric light beam is installed in the steeple of Beverly's First Baptist Church. This is designated as the "Hospital Point Rear Range Light." The lighthouse now is formally known as the "Hospital Point Front Range Light." Mariners now have an additional beacon to improve safety as they enter the harbor.

1928: The IOV is replaced by an electrically powered light.

1939: The Lighthouse Service is absorbed into the U.S. Coast Guard. Keepers are now Coast Guard employees.

1947: Hospital Point Light is automated, using a photocell to automatically turn it on and off depending on the level of light. The last keeper departs the station.

1950: The former keeper's house is designated as the official residence of the commander of the First U.S. Coast Guard District and family.

Postcards, c. 1915 and 1920

APPENDIX TWO
KEEPERS OF THE LIGHTHOUSE 1871 – 1947

(Note: No roster of Massachusetts lighthouse keepers seems to be in print. So we compiled our own for Hospital Point, using city directories at the Beverly Historical Society, along with a couple of online name searches.)

William Augustus Friend, 1871-1873. He appears to have been known locally by his middle name. We have not found out where he came from, and he appears to have left Beverly after 1874.

JOSEPH HENRY HERRICK, 1873-1917

Levi B. Clark, 1917- 1926. JHH's successor had a long and distinguished career with the Lighthouse Service before he was picked for the Beverly post. From what has been learned from online sources, Clark in his early years with the service served as assistant keeper at dreary, storm-tossed Minot's Ledge Light. In 1910-11 he was made keeper of Boston Light. He next appears in charge of the lighthouse on Cuttyhunk Island, most distant in the Elizabeth Islands chain which runs south and west from Wood's Hole and which comprise the town of Gosnold, named for explorer Matthew Gosnold who visited these shores in 1602. Cuttyhunk is the only publicly accessible island and its little village serves as center for Gosnold's government. The small year-round population is bolstered by summer residents and visitors, but it is off the "beaten path." In addition to his lighthouse duties, Clark served as Sunday school superintendent for Cuttyhunk's picturesque village church, fondly called "the little church on the hill," and also was lay reader for Episcopal services held there in the summer. After leaving Beverly in 1926, Clark and his wife Sophie headed for the South Coast again, taking up duties at Woods Hole.

Richard F. Dixon, 1927-1939. Little could be learned about Dixon's career, other than that between 1909 and 1911 he was keeper at Great Point Light on Nantucket. He may have been the man who married Harriett Walker of East Dennis in Barnstable on 23 January, 1904; if so he was born in 1878. Dixon would be the only keeper to die while serving at Hospital Point, on 19 June 1939. His widow, whose name was Harriett, moved to Cummaquid on Cape Cod.

Arthur A. Small, 1939-1947. Small, born in New Bedford, was a former seaman who joined the Lighthouse Service. His hobby was painting, and he compiled a collection of his own art work. The late author-historian Edward Rowe Snow, the renowned friend of lighthouse keepers who for many years as the "Flying Santa" dropped gift bundles from the air to isolated light stations, once called Small "probably the greatest painter who was ever in the Lighthouse Service." In 1922 Small was given one of the tougher assignments in the service, Palmer's Island Light on a tiny isle off New Bedford, where storms could send dangerous waves crashing ashore.

He experienced a great personal tragedy there on September 21, 1938, the day of the Great New England Hurricane, which struck this area with almost no warning. Forecasters in those days lacked the satellite photos and other devices which make hurricane predictions much easier now. They were aware, of course, that a strong hurricane was lurking off the Carolina coast, but they expected it to do what hurricanes were supposed to do, veer out to sea well south of New England. Eastern New England had not been visited by a major hurricane since 1869, an event which only a few old-timers remembered. Official forecasts on the morning of September 21 called for a cloudy day with showers likely. Instead, the monster storm barreled up the coast, crossed Long Island Sound and slammed into the southern coast just east of the Connecticut River valley. This put eastern Connecticut, Rhode Island, eastern Massachusetts and even parts of New Hampshire directly in the path of the easterly part of the storm, where the winds are the most fierce. The result was devastating destruction and loss of life due to the lack of warning. On Palmer's Island, as the storm gained intensity, Arthur Small attempted to walk from the relative safety of the keeper's house to the more exposed lighthouse tower. As he did so, a wave broke over him, knocking him off his feet and threatening to carry him away. His wife Mabel, seeing what was happening to her husband, bravely rushed to the boathouse in hopes of launching a rowboat to rescue him. As she did so, a huge wave broke over the boathouse, destroying it and sweeping Mabel to her death. (Her body was recovered later.) Although badly injured, Keeper Small managed to regain his footing and reached the relative safety of the lighthouse tower. He could, of course, do nothing for his gallant spouse. Through the rest of the day and what must have been a terrible night, Small stood to his duty and kept the light burning. The next day, with the storm gone and the seas subsiding, friends made their way to the island, rescued the keeper and took him to a hospital. Small was given an extended leave of absence to recover.

In the summer of 1939, with the Hospital Point job suddenly open, he was well enough to accept. That year, the Coast Guard took over from the Lighthouse Service, so Arthur Small became a Coast Guard member. He stayed at Hospital Point until the light was automated in 1947, at which time the directory noted that he had relocated to Squantum (Quincy). With him went his son, Allan A. Small, also a member of the Coast Guard, who may have assisted his father during his final months in Beverly.

With his departure, the saga of Hospital Point's lighthouse keepers was complete. Joseph Henry Herrick served more than a decade longer than all of his fellow keepers combined.

APPENDIX THREE
MISERY LOVES COMPANY

In his lighthouse journal, Joseph Henry Herrick made a couple of complimentary references to Daniel Neville of Misery Island for his courage and hospitality in going to the rescue of shipwrecked or stranded sailors. This happened twice in April of 1881. On April 22, Herrick wrote: "Schooner Active went ashore on House Island. Capt. Wilson and crew were saved by Capt. Daniel Neville of Misery Island. Vessel a total wreck." That same month, "Schooner Esther from St. Andrews N.B. (New Brunswick) was wrecked on Misery Island. This crew was also cared for by Capt. Neville and sons." A history of Misery Island by former "island child" Reed Harwood, published in Volume 103 of the Essex Institute Historical Collections (1967) makes reference to Daniel Neville and, citing the writings of Robert Rantoul of Beverly, credits Neville's "lively interest in all the ships and yachts that sailed near the island. He earned the sobriquet of 'Lord of the Isles' and was noted for the numerous occasions on which he went to the rescue of yachtsmen whose boats had capsized or become stranded on a reef."

Daniel Neville, a native of Ireland, took a lease on Misery in 1844, then according to Dr. Harwood, bought it and its small satellite Little Misery from the Dodge family of Wenham in 1849 for $2,900, paying $1,000 down and discharging the mortgage by 1855. After first making his living by quarrying stone, he gave that up and took to farming and fishing on the island. He and his wife Mary raised nine children there. They raised heifers, which the Neville boys would swim behind a dory to West Beach in the fall and march to the market in Salem. At about the time of the rescues referred to by Keeper Herrick, sons Thomas and William were in residence with them on Misery. Daniel Neville died in 1885, leaving the island to his widow.

After surviving the burning of her house in December of 1895, Mary Neville died on Misery in 1897.

In January 1900, daughter Annie Neville sold Misery to a group of Boston speculators, the Misery Island Syndicate, for the astonishing sum of $60,000. They turned the island into a summer membership resort, complete with clubhouse and nine-hole golf course. With debt of $100,000 and membership dues of less than $9,000, it wasn't long until the syndicate went bankrupt. The successor Misery Island Trust, which took over in 1904, fared better and added some cash by selling a few one-acre lots on the island. Some of those owners, including Reed Harwood's father, built private cottages. Supplies came by a steam launch from the pier at West Beach. But after 1916, the Trust also went belly-up. A new group of investors wanted to change the name to "Mystery Island," but faced a triple whammy – the silly name, a nation in the throes of World War I with the threat of German U-boats off the coast, and worst of all, lack of sufficient capital. The resort was closed for good before the summer of 1918, and after 1920 the last of the cottage owners also abandoned Misery. A fire in 1926 destroyed many of the derelict buildings. After it was reported in 1935 that Misery was being eyed as the site for an oil storage terminal, a group of conservation minded North Shore residents bought the abandoned resort and deeded it to the Trustees of Reservations. The Beverly-based Trustees later acquired the last privately owned parcels so the organization now has full title to the Miseries. Within certain rules, the Trustees of Reservations welcomes company.

APPENDIX FOUR
THE 'OTHER' JOSEPH HENRY HERRICK

The lighthouse keeper's uncle, for whom he was named, also enjoyed longevity, living to age 88, and had a varied, interesting career of his own. The first Joseph Henry Herrick, son of Thomas and Mary, was married in Beverly to Lucy Cole on 25 Sept., 1834, a month short of his 22nd birthday. His bride may have been the daughter of Oliver and Polly (Deadman) Cole of Beverly; if so, she was three years older than Joseph. No births of any children to the couple were recorded in Beverly.

Joseph Henry Herrick the elder was for more than two decades a railroad man, in the employ of the Eastern Railroad, which built the first line from East Boston to Salem in 1838, extended it to Beverly the next year, then laid track north to Portsmouth, New Hampshire and Portland, Maine, along with a number of branch lines. Later, the Eastern was taken over by the Boston & Maine. A report in the January 23, 1873 edition of the *Beverly Citizen*, discovered by Fred Hammond, reads:

> Mr. Joseph H. Herrick, after a service of more than a quarter of a century in the employ of the Eastern Railroad Company, retires on the first of February from that service. The close confinement of the ticket office tells upon his health, and he seeks rest and restoration. Mr. Herrick first served the Railroad Company in charge of the switch at the then junction of the Gloucester Branch with the main road near Draper's Point, a place always felt by the railroad officials and by all others familiar therewith to be one of great responsibility. From thence when the new station was built, in the winter of 1854, Mr. Herrick was appointed Station Master, in which

post he continued until about two years ago when he was relieved of all but ticket selling.

So the older JHH may have been the first railroad man forced to retire due to claustrophobia, because he couldn't stand being cooped up in the little ticket booth at the Beverly depot. The job seemingly was having a negative impact on his health. He was 60 years old at the time. For a bit of background: The Eastern opened the Gloucester Branch in 1847 (the extension to Rockport came in 1861), so if Mr. Herrick had more than a quarter of a century of service in January 1873 it stands to reason that he was hired when the branch line opened.

There were no powered switches at that time, of course, so everything had to be thrown by hand. It must have been a tedious job to stand at the junction all day waiting for one of the three or four Gloucester Branch trains on the timetable during the early years. When one approached, the junction guardian had to unlock the switch stand and throw the switch to realign the rail points. Once the train was clear, the switch would have to be re-lined. It certainly was, as the *Citizen* reported, a job of great responsibility, since carelessness by the switch man would send the train headed north toward Maine instead of to Cape Ann, and an improperly lined junction switch would cause a derailment. But after seven years of this, Mr. Herrick must have been ready for a change. The opening of the second Beverly depot in 1854, replacing the original 1839 station down near Congress Street, provided a promotion to station master for the loyal Beverly resident. That building was on the opposite side of the tracks from the third and final Beverly Depot which replaced it more than 40 years later. Draper's Point, according to the list of old place names compiled in 1944 by Stephen J. Connolly, was at the "south end of Beckford

Street." It was also the site of the second landing place for the ferry from Salem that operated before the bridge was built in 1788.

Retirement from the railroad was hardly the end of Mr. Herrick's working life; he'd have plenty to do for nearly three decades afterward. The 1877 Beverly Directory has him operating a provisions store on Railroad Avenue. Five years later he had moved the store to Cabot Street. In 1884, at age 71, he had gone into the milk business. And he also assumed a major responsibility for Beverly, that of overseer of the poor, which the 1893 directory listed as his occupation. It was a major public expenditure. For many years, the town, and city, of Beverly operated an almshouse for persons too poor to care for themselves, and also maintained a sort of temporary welfare system to assist families in financial distress but who could still live on their own. By 1894, the year Beverly changed from town to city government, Joseph H. Herrick was chairman of the Overseers of the Poor. That year the almshouse sheltered and fed 39 paupers, with an average occupancy at any time of 26. In addition, 149 Beverly families received public assistance that year "outside of the almshouse." All of this was administered by the overseers of the poor.

In the Beverly City Documents for 1901, the Board of Overseers concluded its annual report to the voters with these words: "The Chairman of this Board, Mr. Joseph H. Herrick, a most thorough and conscientious man whom all respected, died after serving on this Board for nearly twenty years. His worth is known to no one better than to the members of this Board; his assistance to us in our daily associations has been a great help in conducting this department."

We don't, of course, know what sort of relationship the elder JHH had over the years with his nephew, the keeper of the Hospital Point Lighthouse, but we can hope that when they did see each other it was a cordial reunion. It was after the death of his uncle that the keeper stopped referring to himself as Joseph H. Herrick 2nd. The older man, born 22 years before his namesake, was outlived by 26 years by JHH the younger. Between them they totaled 178 years on this earth.

U.S. Coast Guard Auxiliary:
A Proud Tradition, A Worthy Mission

For over 70 years, tens-of-thousands of men and women of the Coast Guard Auxiliary have spent millions of volunteer hours helping the Coast Guard carry out its mission. They have saved countless lives through their work, on and off the water. Auxiliarists are probably best known for educating the public through their boating safety clasclasses and vessel safety checks. Yet, they do much more. The Coast Guard Authorization Act of 1996 allows the Auxiliary to assist the Coast Guard in performance of any Coast Guard function, duty, role, mission or operation authorized by law and authorized by the Commandant.

When the Coast Guard "Reserve" was authorized by act of Congress on June 23, 1939, the Coast Guard was given a legislative mandate to use civilian volunteers to promote safety on and over the high seas and the nation's navigable waters. The Coast Guard Reserve was then a non-military service comprised of unpaid, volunteer U.S. citizens who owned motorboats or yachts. Two years later, on Feb. 19, Congress amended the 1939 act with passage of the Auxiliary and Reserve Act of 1941. Passage of this act designated the Reserve as a military branch of the active service, while the civilian volunteers, formerly referred to as the Coast Guard Reserve, became the Auxiliary. So, Feb. 19 is formally recognized as the birth of the Coast Guard Reserve while June 23 is recognized as birthday of the Coast Guard Auxiliary.

When America entered World War II, 50,000 Auxiliary members joined the war effort. Some auxiliarists served weeks at a time with the Temporary Reserve. They guarded waterfronts, carried out coastal picket patrols, rescued survivors from scuttled ships and did anything else they were asked to do. Many of their private vessels were placed in service.

After the war, auxiliarists resumed their recreational boating safety duties. The Auxiliary's four cornerstones - Vessel Examination, Education, Operations and Fellowship - were established and remain the Auxiliary's pillars in the 1990s. The Vessel Examination program evolved into the well-known Vessel Safety Check (VSC), a free examination available to any recreational boater. VSCs help boaters ensure their craft complies with Federal regulations regarding safety equipment requirements.

As for education, the Auxiliary teaches boating safety to recreational boaters of all ages. The Auxiliary offers Boating Skills and Seamanship (geared toward power boaters) and sailing courses (for sailboaters) as well as basic and advanced navigation courses.

The Auxiliary operates safety and regatta patrols and is an integral part of the Coast Guard Search and Rescue team. Auxiliarists also assist the Coast Guard with such activities as recreational boating education, vessel safety checks, commercial fishing vessel exams, radio watchstanding, aids to navigation, bridge inspections, and marine environmental inspections. Today, as in 1939, auxiliarists are civilian volunteers who are authorized to wear a uniform similar to the Coast Guard Officer's uniform. Distinctive emblems, buttons, insignias, and ribbons are employed to identify the wearer as a member of the Auxiliary. The Auxiliary has members in all 50 states, Puerto Rico, the Virgin Islands, American Samoa, and Guam. Membership is open to men and women, 17 years or older, U.S. citizens of all states and territories, civilians or active duty or former members of any of the uniformed services and their Reserve components, including the Coast Guard. Facility (radio station, boat or aircraft) ownership is desirable but not mandatory.

Although under the authority of the Commandant of the U.S. Coast Guard, the Auxiliary is internally autonomous, operating on four organizational levels: Flotilla, Division, District Regions and National. The North Shore Division has about 160 members and is made up of five smaller units called Flotillas. They are located in Beverly, Marblehead, Gloucester, Lynn and Danvers. The Division provides support to Station Gloucester and Sector Boston.

In June 2007, the Division formed a Lighthouse Committee and established the Hospital Point Lighthouse Tour Program. The primary objectives of the program are to enhance public access, on a limited basis, to the lighthouse; provide a better understanding and appreciation of the historical significance of the lighthouse tower and grounds; and to provide a public service by providing access to a landmark that is listed on the National Register of Historic Places.

The U.S. Coast Guard Auxiliary is the largest volunteer marine safety organization in the world and has fostered similar ones in foreign countries. During its seventy years, it has lived up to its motto of "A Proud Tradition, A Worthy Mission."

Dedication

This book is dedicated in loving memory of Philip H. Karwowski of Beverly, whose photo of Hospital Point Light appears above. Phil and his wife Deanna, long-time members of the U.S. Coast Guard Auxiliary, were leaders in the 2007 creation of the Hospital Point Lighthouse Tour Program, which has allowed for limited public access to the historic Beverly landmark. Phil also established and hosted a popular series of cable television programs on area lighthouses produced by BEVCAM. His enthusiastic interest in the Beverly Historical Society and its programs was extensive, and he is deeply missed.

www.ingramcontent.com/pod-product-compliance
Lightning Source LLC
Chambersburg PA
CBHW031437040426
42444CB00006B/860